Easy
Bento
Cookbook

Table of Contents

Chicken Teriyaki Bento

Are you looking for an easy and delicious meal to please the whole family? Chicken Teriyaki Bento is a great choice. This popular Japanese dish consists of traditional marinated chicken, white rice, and a variety of tasty side dishes in a bento box. Not only is this meal visually appealing, but it also provides a nourishing combination of protein, carbohydrates, and vegetables.

Ingredients:

- 4 boneless, skinless chicken breasts
- Salt and pepper to taste
- 2 tablespoons cornstarch
- 2 tablespoons vegetable oil
- 1/2 cup soy sauce
- 1/2 cup brown sugar
- 1/4 cup rice vinegar
- 2 cloves garlic, minced
- 1 inch fresh ginger, grated
- 4 green onions, thinly sliced
- Optional: steamed rice and mixed veggies (such as broccoli, carrots, and edamame) for packing

Instructions:

1. Cut the chicken breasts into 1-inch cubes and season with salt and pepper. Place the cornstarch in a shallow dish and coat the chicken cubes in the cornstarch.
2. In a large frying pan, heat the vegetable oil over medium heat. Add the chicken cubes and cook for 5-7 minutes

until fully cooked and golden brown. Remove from the pan and set aside.

3. Whisk together the soy sauce, brown sugar, rice vinegar, garlic, and ginger in a small saucepan. Cook over medium heat until the sugar has dissolved, then set aside.
4. Add the green onions to the same pan used to cook the chicken and cook for 1-2 minutes or until fragrant.
5. Pour the sauce over the chicken cubes and green onions and stir to combine. Cook for 2-3 minutes or until heated through and the sauce has thickened.
6. Place chicken teriyaki, egg, and mixed veggies on top of rice.
7. Pack peaches and strawberries in an open space in the bento box.
8. Cool down completely before closing the bento box cover.

Teriyaki Salmon With Asparagus And Caesar Salad

Are you looking for a delicious, easy-to-make meal that will please the whole family? Look no further than this delectable teriyaki salmon with asparagus and Caesar salad! This unique combination of flavors uses simple ingredients to create an unforgettable taste. Not only is this meal packed with flavor, but it's also filled with numerous health benefits, from the omega-3 fatty acids found in salmon to the vitamin C and fiber found in asparagus.

Teriyaki Salmon With Asparagus
Ingredients:

- 4 salmon fillets, skin on
- 1/4 cup soy sauce
- 2 tablespoons brown sugar
- 2 tablespoons mirin
- 1 tablespoon cornstarch
- 1 tablespoon sesame oil
- 4 cloves garlic, minced
- 2 tablespoons freshly squeezed orange juice
- 2 tablespoons freshly squeezed lemon juice
- Salt and pepper to taste
- 4 heads of asparagus, washed and trimmed
- Optional: steamed rice for packing

Instructions:

1. Whisk together the soy sauce, brown sugar, mirin, cornstarch, sesame oil, garlic, orange juice, lemon juice, salt, and pepper in a small saucepan. Cook the sauce over medium heat, stirring until thick and bubbly. Remove from heat and set aside.
2. Preheat oven to 400°F (200°C). Line a baking sheet with parchment paper.
3. Place the salmon fillets, skin side down, on the prepared baking sheet. Brush both sides of the salmon with the teriyaki sauce.
4. Bake the salmon for 12-15 minutes until fully cooked and flaky.
5. Bring a pot of salted water to a boil in a large saucepan. Add the asparagus and cook for 2-3 minutes until bright green and tender. Drain and set aside.
6. Pack the baked teriyaki salmon and asparagus (with steamed rice, if desired) in the bento box.

Caesar salad

Ingredients:

- 1 head of Romaine lettuce, washed and chopped
- 1/2 cup freshly grated Parmesan cheese
- 1/2 cup croutons
- 2 cloves garlic, minced
- 2 anchovy fillets, chopped (optional)
- 2 tablespoons freshly squeezed lemon juice
- 1 tablespoon Dijon mustard
- 1/2 cup mayonnaise

- 1/2 cup extra-virgin olive oil
- Salt and pepper to taste

Instructions:

1. Mix the chopped Romaine lettuce, grated Parmesan cheese, and croutons in a large bowl.
2. Whisk together the garlic, anchovies (if using), lemon juice, Dijon mustard, mayonnaise, olive oil, salt, and pepper in a small bowl.
3. Pour the dressing over the lettuce mixture and toss to combine.
4. Pack the Caesar salad in an open space in the bento box.

Teriyaki Chicken Meatball Bento

Teriyaki Chicken Meatball Bento is a delicious and nutritious meal of various traditional Japanese ingredients. It's an easy-to-prepare bento box that can be enjoyed for lunch, dinner, or even as a snack. This dish consists of steamed rice, teriyaki chicken meatballs, and various vegetables arranged attractively. The teriyaki sauce adds sweet and savory flavors to the plate, making it even more appealing.

Ingredients:

- 1 pound ground chicken
- 1/2 cup breadcrumbs
- 1 egg
- 2 cloves garlic, minced
- 1/4 cup green onions, thinly sliced
- Salt and pepper to taste
- 2 tablespoons vegetable oil
- 1/2 cup soy sauce
- 1/2 cup brown sugar
- 1/4 cup rice vinegar
- 1 inch fresh ginger, grated
- Optional: steamed rice and mixed veggies (such as broccoli, carrots, and edamame) for packing

Instructions:

1. Mix the ground chicken, breadcrumbs, egg, garlic, green onions, salt, and pepper in a large bowl. Roll the mixture into 1-inch meatballs.

2. In a large frying pan, heat the vegetable oil over medium heat. Add the meatballs and cook for 5-7 minutes or until fully cooked and golden brown on all sides. Remove from the pan and set aside.
3. Whisk together the soy sauce, brown sugar, rice vinegar, and ginger in a small saucepan. Cook over medium heat until the sugar has dissolved, then set aside.
4. In the same pan used to cook the meatballs, pour the sauce over the meatballs and stir to combine. Cook for 2-3 minutes or until heated through and the sauce has thickened.
5. Pack the teriyaki chicken meatballs with steamed rice and mixed veggies (if desired) in the bento box.

Zucchini Noodle Caprese And Baked Chicken Bento

This recipe book is about a delicious and nutritious lunch option that is perfect for anyone who desires variety and flavor. The combination of zucchini noodle caprese and baked chicken bento provides an exciting mix of vegetables, protein, carbohydrates, and flavor. Not only does this meal offer a range of tastes, but it can be prepared in less than thirty minutes! This recipe will become a go-to staple in your weekly meal-planning rotation.

Zucchini Noodle Caprese
Ingredients:

- 2 medium zucchinis
- 2 medium tomatoes
- 1 ball of fresh mozzarella cheese
- 10-12 fresh basil leaves
- 2 tablespoons extra virgin olive oil
- Salt and pepper to taste
- Balsamic glaze, optional

Instructions:

1. Use a spiralizer or a julienne peeler to make zucchini noodles. Place the noodles in a colander and sprinkle with salt to help remove excess moisture. Let them sit for 10-15 minutes.
2. Cut the tomatoes into small pieces. Cut the mozzarella cheese into small cubes.

3. In a large bowl, combine the zucchini noodles, tomatoes, mozzarella cheese, and basil leaves.
4. Drizzle the olive oil over the mixture and season with salt and pepper to taste.
5. Toss the ingredients until everything is evenly coated.
6. Pack the zucchini noodle caprese in the bento box and drizzle with balsamic glaze, if desired.

Baked Chicken

Ingredients:

- 4 boneless, skinless chicken breasts
- Salt and pepper to taste
- 1 tablespoon extra virgin olive oil
- 2 cloves of garlic, minced
- 1/4 teaspoon dried thyme
- 1/4 teaspoon dried oregano

Instructions:

1. Preheat the oven to 400°F (200°C).
2. Season the chicken breasts with salt and pepper.
3. In a large oven-safe skillet, heat the olive oil over medium heat.
4. Add the chicken breasts to the skillet and cook for 2-3 minutes on each side until they are browned.
5. Remove the skillet from the heat and add the minced garlic, thyme, and oregano to the skillet.
6. Place the skillet in the oven and bake the chicken for 20-25 minutes, or until the internal temperature of the chicken reaches 165°F (74°C).

7. Let the chicken rest for 5-10 minutes before packing.
8. Pack the baked chicken in an open space in the bento box.

Tuna Salad Sandwich And Watermelon Tomato Salad

The tuna salad sandwich and watermelon tomato salad will make your mouth water! With its simple ingredients and minimal preparation time, this meal is perfect for a family on the go. The combination of healthy vegetables and fresh fruits provides a unique flavor that is delicious and nutritious. Plus, the leftovers can be used to create multiple other dishes, making it an economical choice.

Tuna Salad Sandwich

Ingredients:

- 2 cans of tuna, drained
- 1/4 cup mayonnaise
- 1/4 cup diced celery
- 1/4 cup diced red onion
- 2 tablespoons sweet pickle relish
- Salt and pepper to taste
- 8 slices of bread
- Lettuce leaves, optional
- Tomato slices, optional

Instructions:

1. Mix the tuna, mayonnaise, celery, red onion, and sweet pickle relish in a medium-sized bowl.
2. Season with salt and pepper to taste.
3. Toast the bread slices until they are golden brown.
4. Spread the tuna mixture evenly on 4 slices of bread.

5. Top each with a lettuce leaf and a tomato slice, if desired.
6. Close each sandwich by placing the remaining slices of bread on top of the fillings.
7. Pack the sandwich in the bento box.

Watermelon Tomato Salad

Ingredients:

- 4 cups diced seedless watermelon
- 2 cups cherry tomatoes, halved
- 1/2 red onion, thinly sliced
- 1/4 cup fresh basil leaves, chopped
- 2 tablespoons extra virgin olive oil
- 2 tablespoons balsamic vinegar
- Salt and pepper to taste

Instructions:

1. Mix the diced watermelon, cherry tomatoes, red onion, and basil leaves in a large bowl.
2. In a small bowl, whisk together the olive oil and balsamic vinegar.
3. Pour the dressing over the watermelon mixture and gently toss to combine.
4. Season with salt and pepper to taste.
5. Cover and refrigerate the salad for at least 30 minutes before packing to allow the flavors to develop.
6. Pack the watermelon tomato salad in an open space in the bento box.

7. You can also add other ingredients like feta cheese, chopped nuts, or fresh mint leaves to add more flavor and texture to the salad.

Pasta Salad Bento

Pasta salad is an easy yet delicious and nutritious meal everyone can enjoy. In addition, Bento boxes are a fun way to enjoy meals in a creative and organized fashion. With the combination of these two popular items, pasta salad bento is the perfect combination of convenience, nutrition, and presentation. This article will overview pasta salad bento, tips for creating your version at home, helpful meal-planning ideas, and more.

Ingredients:

- 8 oz. of your favorite pasta shape
- 1 cup cherry tomatoes, halved
- 1/2 cup sliced cucumber
- 1/2 cup diced red bell pepper
- 1/4 cup diced red onion
- 1/4 cup chopped fresh parsley
- 2 tablespoons extra virgin olive oil
- 2 tablespoons red wine vinegar
- Salt and pepper to taste
- Optional: crumbled feta cheese, sliced black olives, or grilled chicken for added protein

Instructions:

1. Cook the pasta according to the package instructions until al dente. Drain and rinse with cold water to cool.
2. Mix the cooked pasta, cherry tomatoes, cucumber, red bell pepper, red onion, and parsley in a large bowl.

3. Whisk together the olive oil and red wine vinegar in a small bowl.
4. Pour the dressing over the pasta mixture and gently toss to combine.
5. Season with salt and pepper to taste.
6. Cover and refrigerate the pasta salad for at least 30 minutes before packing to allow the flavors to develop.
7. Pack the pasta salad in a bento box.
8. For added flavor and protein, you can add other ingredients like crumbled feta cheese, sliced black olives, or grilled chicken.

Smoked Salmon Pinwheels And Melon Salad

Smoked Salmon Pinwheels are a delicious and easy appetizer that everyone can enjoy. Not only are they simple to make, but they also look impressive when served. These tasty pinwheels are flavorful due to the smoked salmon, cream cheese, and fresh dill. The combination of ingredients creates an irresistible bite that is perfect for any occasion.

Ingredients:

- 4 oz. of smoked salmon, sliced
- 2 cups diced cantaloupe or honeydew melon
- 1/2 cup diced red onion
- 1/4 cup chopped fresh dill
- 2 tablespoons freshly squeezed lemon juice
- Salt and pepper to taste
- Mixed greens or arugula for packing

Instructions:

1. Mix the smoked salmon, cantaloupe, honeydew melon, red onion, and dill in a large bowl.
2. Whisk the lemon juice, salt, and pepper in a small bowl.
3. Pour the lemon dressing over the salmon mixture and gently toss to combine.
4. Cover and refrigerate the salad for at least 30 minutes before packing to allow the flavors to develop.
5. Pack the smoked salmon and melon salad over a bed of mixed greens or arugula.
6. Start packing cooled foods into the bento box.

7. For added flavor and texture, you can add other ingredients like crumbled feta cheese, sliced cucumber, or cherry tomatoes.

Mediterranean Bento Lunch

The Mediterranean diet has been highly praised for its health benefits, and it can be easily enjoyed in a delicious lunchtime bento. A bento box is an ideal way to create a balanced meal that celebrates the flavors of the Mediterranean region. This article will explore what makes up a Mediterranean bento lunch, how to assemble one, and some creative ideas for adding variety to your meals.

Ingredients:

- 1 cup cooked quinoa or brown rice
- 1 cup cherry tomatoes, halved
- 1/2 cup sliced cucumber
- 1/2 cup diced red bell pepper
- 1/4 cup pitted Kalamata olives
- 1/4 cup crumbled feta cheese
- 2 tablespoons freshly squeezed lemon juice
- 2 tablespoons extra virgin olive oil
- Salt and pepper to taste
- Optional: grilled chicken or tofu for added protein

Instructions:

1. Mix the cooked quinoa or brown rice, cherry tomatoes, cucumber, red bell pepper, Kalamata olives, and feta cheese in a large bowl.
2. Whisk together the lemon juice, olive oil, salt, and pepper in a small bowl.
3. Pour the lemon dressing over the rice mixture and gently toss to combine.

4. Cover and refrigerate the rice salad for at least 30 minutes before packing to allow the flavors to develop.
5. Pack the Mediterranean rice salad in a bento box with grilled chicken or tofu for added protein, if desired.
6. For added flavor and texture, you can add other ingredients like sliced red onion, chopped parsley, or sliced avocado.

Baked Miso Salmon Rice And Prawn, Mango, and Avocado Salad

Are you looking for a delicious and nutritious meal? Look no further. Baked Miso Salmon Rice is an easy yet flavorful dish that can be prepared in just one hour. This hearty and filling meal combines two classic Japanese ingredients, salmon and miso paste, with fragrant jasmine rice to make a balanced dinner that will satisfy your taste buds.

Baked Miso Salmon Rice

Ingredients:

- 4 salmon fillets, skin removed
- 1/4 cup miso paste
- 2 tablespoons mirin
- 2 tablespoons sake
- 2 tablespoons brown sugar
- 2 tablespoons freshly squeezed lemon juice
- Salt and pepper to taste
- 2 cups cooked short-grain rice
- 1/2 cup edamame, shelled
- 1/2 cup cherry tomatoes, halved
- 1/4 cup sliced green onions

Instructions:

1. Preheat oven to 400°F (200°C). Line a baking sheet with parchment paper.
2. Whisk together the miso paste, mirin, sake, brown sugar, lemon juice, salt, and pepper in a small bowl.

3. Place the salmon fillets on the prepared baking sheet and brush both sides with the miso mixture.
4. Bake the salmon for 12-15 minutes until fully cooked and flaky.
5. Mix the cooked rice, edamame, cherry tomatoes, and green onions in a large bowl.
6. Pack the baked miso salmon and rice mixture in a bento box.

Prawn, Mango, And Avocado Salad

Ingredients:

- 1 lb. cooked prawns, peeled and deveined
- 2 ripe mangoes, peeled and diced
- 2 ripe avocados, diced
- 1/2 red onion, thinly sliced
- 1/4 cup chopped fresh cilantro
- 2 tablespoons freshly squeezed lime juice
- Salt and pepper to taste
- Mixed greens or arugula for packing

Instructions:

1. Mix the cooked prawns, mango, avocado, red onion, and cilantro in a large bowl.
2. Whisk together the lime juice, salt, and pepper in a small bowl.
3. Pour the lime dressing over the prawn mixture and gently toss to combine.
4. Cover and refrigerate the salad for at least 30 minutes before packing to allow the flavors to develop.

5. Pack the prawn, mango, and avocado salad in an open space in the bento box.
6. This bento box is best packed warm but can also be enjoyed cold. For added flavor and texture, you can add other ingredients like sliced cucumber, pickled ginger, or sesame seeds.

Pesto And Egg Baguette Sandwich

If you're looking for a quick and delicious lunch or dinner option, look no further than this tasty Pesto And Egg Baguette Sandwich. This sandwich is easy to make and requires only a few ingredients, making it perfect for any busy day. It has all the flavors of a classic pesto dish but with the bonus of eggs for extra protein. Plus, it's packed with fresh herbs and vegetables to give it an extra nutritional boost.

Ingredients:

- 1 baguette, sliced lengthwise
- 4 large eggs
- 2 tablespoons butter
- 1/2 cup prepared pesto
- Salt and pepper to taste
- 4 slices of cheese (cheddar, mozzarella, or any cheese of your choice)
- Optional: sliced tomatoes, lettuce, or bacon for packing

Instructions:

1. Preheat oven to 375°F (190°C).
2. Place the sliced baguette on a baking sheet and spread the pesto on both sides.
3. In a large frying pan, melt the butter over medium heat. Crack in the eggs and cook until set, about 3-4 minutes.
4. Place the cooked eggs on half the baguette and sprinkle with salt and pepper.
5. Add the cheese slices on top of the eggs.

6. Bake the baguette in the oven for 5-7 minutes or until the cheese is melted and bubbly.
7. Pack the pesto and egg baguette sandwich with sliced tomatoes, lettuce, or bacon (if desired) in the bento box.
8. For added flavor and texture, you can also pack additional bento fillers such as sausages, ham, vegetables, and fruits. Enjoy!.

Tropical Jerk Chicken And Gingered Broccoli

Are you looking for an exciting, flavorful twist on traditional chicken dishes? Look no further than tropical jerk chicken! This irresistible dish combines the spicy heat of jerk seasoning with the sweet and sour tang of tropical fruits. Perfect for a summer barbecue or a cozy night in, this dish is sure to please everyone at the table. So whether you're adding it to your weekly meal rotation or making it for special occasions, this Caribbean-inspired dish is sure to have you return for more.

Ingredients:

- 4 boneless, skinless chicken breasts
- 2 tablespoons Jamaican jerk seasoning
- 2 tablespoons olive oil
- 1 head of broccoli, chopped into florets
- 2 tablespoons freshly grated ginger
- 2 cloves garlic, minced
- 1/4 cup freshly squeezed lime juice
- Salt and pepper to taste

Instructions:

1. Mix the Jamaican jerk seasoning and olive oil in a large bowl. Add the chicken breasts and toss to coat.
2. Bring a pot of salted water to a boil in a large saucepan. Add the broccoli florets and cook for 2-3 minutes until bright green and tender. Drain and set aside.

3. Heat a little olive oil over medium heat in a large frying pan. Add the grated ginger and minced garlic and cook for 1-2 minutes or until fragrant.

4. Add the cooked broccoli to the frying pan and toss to combine with the ginger and garlic.

5. Add the lime juice, salt, and pepper to the frying pan and cook for another 2-3 minutes or until the flavors have melded together.

6. Heat a little olive oil over medium heat in a separate large frying pan. Cook the chicken breasts for 4-5 minutes on each side or until fully cooked and golden brown.

7. Pack the tropical jerk chicken with the gingered broccoli (and steamed rice, if desired) in the bento box.

8. You can also pack additional bento fillers such as sweet potatoes, vegetables, and fruits.

Crispy Salmon Bento

Salmon bento is one of the most delicious and nutritious meals available. Not only is it a great way to enjoy some sustainably-sourced salmon, but it also looks beautiful. And if you like your salmon with a bit of crunch, this Crispy Salmon Bento recipe is sure to please. This easy-to-make bento box combines crispy salmon fillets with various vegetables and a flavorful dressing - making it perfect for lunch or dinner.

Ingredients:

- 4 salmon fillets
- 1 cup panko breadcrumbs
- 1/2 cup all-purpose flour
- 2 large eggs, beaten
- Salt and pepper to taste
- Oil for frying
- Optional: steamed rice, mixed greens, or roasted vegetables for packing

Instructions:

1. Set up a breading station by placing the panko breadcrumbs, flour, and beaten eggs in separate shallow dishes. Season each dish with salt and pepper.
2. Pat, the salmon fillets dry with paper towels.
3. Dredge each salmon fillet in the flour, the beaten eggs, and the panko breadcrumbs, and coat each fillet well.
4. In a large frying pan, heat enough oil to cover the bottom of the pan over medium heat.

5. When the oil is hot, carefully place the breaded salmon fillets in the pan and cook for 3-4 minutes on each side until golden brown and crispy.
6. Remove the salmon fillets from the pan and place them on a paper towel-lined plate to drain any excess oil.
7. Pack the crispy salmon with steamed rice, mixed greens, or roasted vegetables (if desired) in the bento box.
8. Add other ingredients like avocado, edamame, or pickled vegetables for added flavor and texture. Enjoy!

Salmon Pasta In Parmesan Cream Sauce

If you're looking for an easy, delicious dinner to make for your family, look no further than Salmon Pasta in Parmesan Cream Sauce. This simple and flavorful dish will have you ready to serve in no time. Bursting with garlic, butter, and Parmesan cheese flavors, this creamy sauce will have everyone asking for seconds. You can find all the ingredients you need at any local grocery store, and it's sure to be a hit with adults and kids alike.

Ingredients:

- 8 ounces of pasta of your choice
- 4 salmon fillets
- Salt and pepper to taste
- 2 tablespoons olive oil
- 3 cloves garlic, minced
- 1 cup heavy cream
- 1/2 cup grated parmesan cheese
- 2 tablespoons freshly squeezed lemon juice
- 1/4 teaspoon red pepper flakes (optional)
- 2 tablespoons chopped fresh parsley

Instructions:

1. Cook the pasta according to the package instructions until al dente. Repack 1/2 cup of the pasta water and set aside.
2. Season the salmon fillets with salt and pepper. Heat 1 tablespoon of olive oil over medium heat in a large frying pan. Cook the salmon fillets on each side for 3-4

minutes or until fully cooked and golden brown. Remove from the pan and set aside.

3. Heat the remaining 1 tablespoon of olive oil in the same pan over medium heat. Add the minced garlic and cook for 1-2 minutes or until fragrant.

4. Pour in the heavy cream, grated parmesan cheese, lemon juice, red pepper flakes (if using), and repacked pasta water. Stir to combine.

5. Bring the sauce to a simmer and cook for 3-5 minutes until the sauce thickens and the cheese has melted.

6. Cut the salmon into bite-sized pieces and add them to the sauce. Toss to combine.

7. Drain the cooked pasta and add it to the pan with the sauce and salmon. Toss to combine.

8. Pack the salmon pasta in parmesan cream sauce with a sprinkle of chopped parsley on top in the bento box and put some fruits and vegetables in the space.

Fiesta Salmon Rice

This Fiesta Salmon Rice is a delicious and nutritious meal for the whole family. It's an easy, one-pot meal with plenty of bold flavors sure to please everyone! This dish combines salmon fillets with fragrant jasmine rice, crisp bell peppers, zesty lime juice, and a variety of seasonings for a flavorful combination.

Ingredients:

- 1 cup long-grain white rice
- 1 and 1/2 cups water
- 1 teaspoon salt
- 2 tablespoons olive oil
- 1 medium onion, diced
- 3 cloves garlic, minced
- 1 red bell pepper, diced
- 1 yellow bell pepper, diced
- 1 cup corn kernels (fresh or frozen)
- 1 cup canned black beans, rinsed and drained
- 1/2 teaspoon chili powder
- 1/2 teaspoon cumin
- 4 salmon fillets
- Salt and pepper to taste
- Optional: cilantro, lime wedges, and sour cream for packing

Instructions:

1. Rinse the rice in a fine-mesh strainer and place it in a saucepan with water and salt. Bring to a boil, reduce the heat to low, cover, and cook for 18-20 minutes, or until

the rice is fully cooked and the water has been absorbed.

2. Heat 1 tablespoon of olive oil over medium heat in a large frying pan. Add the onion, garlic, red bell pepper, yellow bell pepper, corn, black beans, chili powder, and cumin. Cook for 5-7 minutes until the vegetables are tender and fragrant.

3. Season the salmon fillets with salt and pepper. Heat the remaining 1 tablespoon of olive oil over medium heat in a separate frying pan. Cook the salmon fillets on each side for 3-4 minutes or until fully cooked and golden brown. Remove from the pan and set aside.

4. Cut the salmon into bite-sized pieces and add it to the pan with the cooked vegetables. Toss to combine.

5. Stir in the cooked rice and continue to cook for 2-3 minutes or until everything is heated.

6. Pack the fiesta salmon rice with cilantro, lime wedges, and sour cream (if desired) in the bento box and put some fruits and vegetables in the space.

Spam Musubi Bento

Spam Musubi Bento is a delicious Hawaiian snack that has grown in popularity over the years. It consists of a block of rice, Spam, and nori (seaweed) wrapped together in a convenient bundle. This combination of flavors makes it both sweet and savory, with a unique flavor profile that cannot be found anywhere else.

Ingredients:

- 3 cups sushi rice
- 4 tablespoons rice vinegar
- 2 tablespoons sugar
- 1 teaspoon salt
- 4 sheets of nori (dried seaweed)
- 4 slices of Spam
- 3 tablespoons soy sauce
- 2 tablespoons brown sugar
- 1 teaspoon grated ginger
- 1 clove garlic, minced
- Optional: pickled ginger, wasabi, and soy sauce for packing

Instructions:

1. Rinse the sushi rice and drain well. Place in a saucepan with 3 cups of water. Bring to a boil, then reduce heat to low, cover, and simmer for 18-20 minutes or until the water has been absorbed and the rice is tender.

2. Mix the rice vinegar, sugar, and salt in a small bowl. Pour the mixture over the cooked rice and stir to combine. Allow the rice to cool to room temperature.
3. Mix the soy sauce, brown sugar, ginger, and garlic in a small saucepan. Cook over medium heat until the sugar has dissolved and the sauce has thickened about 3-5 minutes.
4. Heat a frying pan over medium heat. Add the Spam and cook on each side for 1-2 minutes until browned and crisp. Remove from the pan and drain on paper towels.
5. Cut each slice of Spam in half lengthwise.
6. Lay out a sheet of nori on a flat surface. Place 1 cup of sushi rice on top of the nori, spreading it evenly, leaving a 1/2-inch border at the top.
7. Place 2 halves of Spam on top of the rice. Spoon a little of the soy sauce mixture over the Spam.
8. Roll the nori tightly around the rice and Spam to form a cylinder.
9. Repeat the process with the remaining nori, rice, Spam, and soy sauce mixture to form 4 musubi.
10. Pack the musubi warm with pickled ginger, wasabi, and soy sauce (if desired) in the bento box.
11. You can also pack additional bento fillers such as sausages, vegetables, and fruits.

Honey Soy Sauce Chicken Bento

Japanese bento boxes are a traditional and delicious way to enjoy an array of flavors in one compact meal. For today's recipe, we're making a Honey Soy Sauce Chicken Bento that will satisfy your taste buds with its sweet and savory flavors. In addition, this dish is easy to make, requiring only a few simple ingredients that you may already have on hand.

Ingredients:

- 4 boneless, skinless chicken thighs
- 3 tablespoons honey
- 2 tablespoons soy sauce
- 1 tablespoon rice vinegar
- 1 tablespoon sake or dry white wine
- 1 tablespoon brown sugar
- 1 teaspoon grated ginger
- 1 clove garlic, minced
- 3 cups cooked Japanese-style white rice
- 3 tablespoons sesame seeds
- Optional: furikake (rice seasoning), pickled vegetables, and seaweed for packing

Instructions:

1. Mix the honey, soy sauce, rice vinegar, sake or wine, brown sugar, ginger, and garlic in a large bowl.
2. Add the chicken thighs to the bowl and toss to coat evenly—Marinate in the refrigerator for at least 30 minutes or up to 2 hours.

3. Preheat the oven to 375°F (190°C). Line a baking sheet with parchment paper.
4. Place the chicken thighs on the prepared baking sheet and bake for 20-25 minutes or until cooked through and the glaze is golden brown.
5. In a small pan, toast the sesame seeds over medium heat until golden brown, about 2-3 minutes.
6. Place chicken thighs on top of rice in the bento box. And it drizzles any remaining glaze over the chicken.
7. Sprinkle the sesame seeds over the chicken.
8. Add any desired furikake, pickled vegetables, or seaweed to the side.
9. You can put some fruits and vegetables in the space.

Rainbow Salmon Skewers And Caesar Salad

If you're looking for an easy and flavorful dinner option, look no further than rainbow salmon skewers and Caesar salad. This dish is a great way to serve fresh fish in a tasty marinade that will tantalize your taste buds. The marinade takes just minutes to throw together, and the skewers can be prepped ahead of time so that all you have to do when you're ready to cook is toss them on the grill or bake them in the oven.

Rainbow Salmon Skewers

Ingredients:

- 4 salmon fillets cut into 1-inch cubes
- Salt and pepper to taste
- 1 red bell pepper, seeded and cut into 1-inch pieces
- 1 yellow bell pepper, seeded and cut into 1-inch pieces
- 1 orange bell pepper, seeded and cut into 1-inch pieces
- 1 small red onion, cut into 1-inch pieces
- 2 tablespoons olive oil
- 2 tablespoons freshly squeezed lemon juice
- 2 cloves garlic, minced
- 2 teaspoons dried oregano
- 8 bamboo skewers (soaked in water for 30 minutes)
- Optional: lemon wedges for packing

Instructions:

1. Preheat your grill or grill pan to medium-high heat.
2. Season the salmon cubes with salt and pepper.

3. Whisk the olive oil, lemon juice, garlic, and oregano in a small bowl.
4. Thread the salmon cubes, red bell pepper, yellow bell pepper, orange bell pepper, and red onion onto the skewers, alternating between each ingredient.
5. Brush the skewers with the lemon and garlic mixture.
6. Place the skewers on the preheated grill or grill pan and cook for 5-7 minutes on each side until the salmon is fully cooked and the vegetables are charred and tender.
7. Pack the rainbow salmon skewers into the bento box.

Caesar Salad

Ingredients:

- 1 head of Romaine lettuce, washed and chopped
- 1/2 cup freshly grated Parmesan cheese
- 1/2 cup croutons
- 2 cloves garlic, minced
- 2 anchovy fillets, chopped (optional)
- 2 tablespoons freshly squeezed lemon juice
- 1 tablespoon Dijon mustard
- 1/2 cup mayonnaise
- 1/2 cup extra-virgin olive oil
- Salt and pepper to taste

Instructions:

1. Mix the chopped Romaine lettuce, grated Parmesan cheese, and croutons in a large bowl.

2. Whisk together the garlic, anchovies (if using), lemon juice, Dijon mustard, mayonnaise, olive oil, salt, and pepper in a small bowl.
3. Pour the dressing over the lettuce mixture and toss to combine.
4. Pack the Caesar salad in an open space in the bento box.
5. For added flavor and protein, you can add other ingredients like boiled eggs, grilled chicken, or bacon. Enjoy!

Salmon Fried Rice

Salmon Fried Rice is an easy and delicious meal that can be made in no time. Perfect for busy weeknights or a quick lunch, this classic Asian dish is a great way to make use of leftovers from the night before. So whether you're cooking for one or feeding a crowd, this flavorful salmon fried rice recipe is sure to be a hit. With only five ingredients and minimal prep time, you'll have dinner in under 30 minutes.

Ingredients:

- 2 cups cooked long-grain white rice
- 4 salmon fillets, cut into 1/2-inch cubes
- Salt and pepper to taste
- 2 tablespoons vegetable oil
- 2 cloves garlic, minced
- 1 small onion, diced
- 2 carrots, peeled and diced
- 2 stalks of celery, diced
- 2 tablespoons soy sauce
- 2 tablespoons oyster sauce
- 1 teaspoon sesame oil
- 2 eggs, lightly beaten
- 2 green onions, thinly sliced
- Optional: sesame seeds and chopped cilantro for packing

Instructions:

1. In a large frying pan, heat 1 tablespoon of vegetable oil over medium heat. Add the salmon cubes and season

with salt and pepper. Cook for 2-3 minutes on each side until fully cooked and golden brown. Remove from the pan and set aside.

2. In the same pan, heat the remaining 1 tablespoon of vegetable oil. Add the garlic, onion, carrots, and celery. Cook for 5-7 minutes until the vegetables are tender and fragrant.

3. Stir in the cooked rice and cook for 2-3 minutes or until heated.

4. Whisk together the soy sauce, oyster sauce, and sesame oil in a small bowl. Pour the sauce over the rice and vegetables, and stir to combine.

5. Push the rice and vegetables to one side of the pan, and pour the beaten eggs onto the other. Scramble the eggs until fully cooked, then mix them into the rice and vegetables.

6. Stir in the cooked salmon cubes and green onions. Cook for 2-3 minutes or until everything is heated through.

7. Pack the salmon fried rice with sesame seeds and cilantro in the bento box.

8. Pack additional bento fillers such as salad, vegetables, and fruits.

Tonkatsu Bento

Tonkatsu bento is a popular Japanese lunch box dish. It is filled with various flavorful ingredients, making it an excellent meal for any occasion. This article will give an in-depth overview of tonkatsu bento, including its essential components and how to put it together. Tonkatsu is this dish's main component, consisting of a deep-fried pork cutlet.

Ingredients:

- 4 pork cutlets
- Salt and pepper to taste
- 2 eggs, beaten
- 1 cup panko breadcrumbs
- 1/2 cup all-purpose flour
- Vegetable oil for frying
- 1 cup tonkatsu sauce (available at Asian supermarkets or online)
- Optional: steamed rice and mixed veggies (such as broccoli, carrots, and edamame) for packing

Instructions:

1. Season the pork cutlets with salt and pepper on both sides.
2. Place the beaten eggs in a shallow dish and the panko breadcrumbs in a separate shallow dish.
3. Dust the pork cutlets in the flour, dip them into the beaten eggs and finally coat them in the panko breadcrumbs.

4. Heat 1/2 inch vegetable oil over medium heat in a large frying pan. Add the pork cutlets and cook on each side for 5-7 minutes until fully cooked and golden brown. Remove from the pan and drain on paper towels.
5. Place tonkatsu with tonkatsu sauce on top of the rice.
6. Pack mixed veggies in an open space in the bento box.
7. You can put some fruits and vegetables in the space.
8. Cool down completely before closing the bento box cover.

Ginger Pork Onigirazu

Ginger Pork Onigirazu is a delicious and unique twist on the traditional Japanese rice ball or onigiri. This savory snack is perfect for a quick meal or as finger food for parties. In addition, it's a great way to mix up your usual lunch routine! You can make this delicious dish with just a few simple ingredients in no time.

Ingredients:

- 1/2 pound ground pork
- 2 tablespoons vegetable oil
- 1/4 cup green onions, thinly sliced
- 1 clove garlic, minced
- 1 inch fresh ginger, grated
- 2 tablespoons soy sauce
- 2 tablespoons brown sugar
- Salt and pepper to taste
- 4 sheets of nori (dried seaweed)
- 4 cups cooked sushi rice
- Optional: pickled ginger, wasabi, and soy sauce for packing

Instructions:

1. In a large frying pan, heat the vegetable oil over medium heat. Add the ground pork, green onions, garlic, and ginger until the pork is browned and cooked, about 5-7 minutes.
2. Mix the soy sauce, brown sugar, salt, and pepper in a small bowl. Pour the mixture over the cooked pork and

stir to combine. Cook for 2-3 minutes or until heated through and the sauce has thickened.

3. Lay out a sheet of nori on a flat surface. Place 1 cup of cooked sushi rice on top of the nori, spreading it evenly, leaving a 1/2-inch border at the top.

4. Spoon 1/4 of the ginger pork mixture on top of the rice.

5. Fold the top border of the nori over the filling, then fold in the sides of the nori to form a square.

6. Repeat the process with the remaining nori, rice, and pork mixture to form 4 onigiris.

7. If desired, pack the onigiris in the bento box with pickled ginger, wasabi, and soy sauce.

8. You can also pack additional bento fillers such as sausages, vegetables, and fruits.

Karaage Bento

Karaage Bento is a popular Japanese dish consisting of fried chicken, rice, and other sides. The perfect combination of flavors and textures makes it an ideal meal choice for lunch or dinner. In addition, the dish is easy to prepare and can be customized to suit your tastes. So whether you're looking for a delicious yet simple lunch option or a uniquely Japanese experience, karaage bento will satisfy you!

Ingredients:

- 1 pound boneless, skinless chicken thighs cut into bite-sized pieces
- 1 cup all-purpose flour
- 1 teaspoon baking powder
- 1 teaspoon salt
- 1/2 teaspoon black pepper
- 1 cup cold club soda
- Vegetable oil for frying
- 3 cups cooked Japanese-style white rice
- Optional: furikake (rice seasoning), pickled vegetables, and seaweed for packing

Instructions:

1. Mix the flour, baking powder, salt, and pepper in a large bowl.
2. Add the club soda to the bowl and stir until a batter forms.
3. Add the chicken pieces to the batter and toss to coat evenly.

4. Heat about 2 inches of oil in a heavy-bottomed pot over medium-high heat until it reaches 350°F (175°C).
5. Working in batches, carefully add the chicken pieces to the hot oil and fry until golden brown and crispy, about 3-5 minutes.
6. Remove the chicken from the oil with a slotted spoon and drain on a paper towel-lined plate.
7. Place karaage chicken on top of the rice in the bento box.
8. Add any desired furikake, pickled vegetables, or seaweed to the side.
9. You can put some fruits and vegetables in the space.

Hamburger Steak Bento

Hamburger steak bento is a simple yet delicious meal perfect for any occasion. It's a popular lunchbox dish in Japan, but anyone worldwide can enjoy it. Not only does it taste great, but it's also surprisingly easy to make. With just a few ingredients and creative seasoning, you can create a delicious bento box with your family or friends begging for more.

Ingredients:

- 1 pound ground beef
- 1/2 cup breadcrumbs
- 1 large egg
- 1 small onion, finely chopped
- 1 clove garlic, minced
- 1 teaspoon salt
- 1/2 teaspoon black pepper
- 1/4 cup all-purpose flour
- 1 tablespoon vegetable oil
- 1 cup beef broth
- 2 tablespoons Worcestershire sauce
- 2 tablespoons tomato ketchup
- 2 tablespoons soy sauce
- 3 cups cooked Japanese-style white rice
- Optional: furikake (rice seasoning), pickled vegetables, and seaweed for packing

Instructions:

1. Mix the ground beef, breadcrumbs, egg, onion, garlic, salt, and pepper in a large bowl.

2. Shape the mixture into 4 equal-sized patties.
3. Place the flour in a shallow dish and dredge each patty in the flour.
4. Heat the oil in a large skillet over medium-high heat.
5. Add the patties to the skillet and cook until browned on both sides, about 3-5 minutes per side.
6. Whisk together the beef broth, Worcestershire sauce, tomato ketchup, and soy sauce in a small bowl.
7. Pour the sauce over the patties in the skillet and bring to a simmer.
8. Reduce the heat to low and continue to cook until the sauce has thickened and the patties are fully cooked about 10 minutes.
9. Place hamburger steak on top of rice in the bento box.
10. Add any desired furikake, pickled vegetables, or seaweed to the side.
11. You can put some fruits and vegetables in the space.

Asparagus Beef Rolls Bento

Asparagus Beef Rolls Bento is a delicious and easy-to-make dish that is perfect for any occasion. This traditional Japanese recipe combines juicy beef, crisp asparagus, and fluffy white rice to make a flavorful meal. Not only is the taste of this bento box delightful, but it also looks beautiful with its colorful ingredients and presentation. Additionally, Asparagus Beef Rolls Bento can be enjoyed in one sitting or portioned into individual meals for the whole family.

Ingredients:

- 8 thin slices of sirloin steak
- 8 asparagus spears, trimmed
- Salt and pepper, to taste
- 4 teaspoons soy sauce
- 4 teaspoons oyster sauce
- 4 teaspoons sake (Japanese rice wine)
- 4 teaspoons mirin (sweet Japanese rice wine)
- 4 teaspoons cornstarch
- 4 teaspoons water
- 3 tablespoons vegetable oil, divided
- 3 cups cooked Japanese-style white rice
- Optional: furikake (rice seasoning), pickled vegetables, and seaweed for packing

Instructions:

1. Place each slice of sirloin steak between two pieces of plastic wrap and gently pound with a meat mallet or rolling pin until thin.

2. Season the steak with salt and pepper.
3. Place one asparagus spear at one end of each slice of steak.
4. Roll the steak around the asparagus, securing it with toothpicks if necessary.
5. Whisk together the soy sauce, oyster sauce, sake, mirin, cornstarch, and water in a small bowl.
6. Heat 2 tablespoons of oil in a large skillet over medium-high heat.
7. Add the beef rolls to the skillet and cook until browned on all sides, about 3-5 minutes.
8. Pour the sauce over the beef rolls in the skillet and bring to a simmer.
9. Reduce the heat to low and continue to cook until the sauce has thickened and the beef rolls are fully cooked about 5 minutes.
10. Place Asparagus Beef Rolls on top of rice in the bento box.
11. Add any desired furikake, pickled vegetables, or seaweed to the side.
12. You can put some fruits and vegetables in the space.

Shrimp And Vegetable Tempura Bento

Tempura Bento is a classic Japanese meal that is quickly becoming popular worldwide. This dish contains various ingredients wrapped up in a neat and tasty package. Tempura Bento combines vegetables, seafood, or other proteins deep-fried in a light batter and served with steamed rice. It can also be done with pickles and other side dishes to provide additional flavor and texture to the meal.

Ingredients:

- 1 cup all-purpose flour
- 1 teaspoon baking powder
- 1 large egg, beaten
- 1 cup ice-cold water
- 1 cup tempura flour
- 1 teaspoon salt
- Oil for frying
- 8 large shrimp, peeled and deveined
- 2 carrots, sliced into rounds
- 2 zucchinis, sliced into rounds
- 2 sweet potatoes, peeled and sliced into rounds
- 3 cups cooked Japanese-style white rice
- Optional: furikake (rice seasoning), pickled vegetables, and seaweed for packing

Instructions:

1. In a large bowl, whisk together the all-purpose flour and baking powder.
2. Add the egg and mix until smooth.

3. Slowly pour in the ice-cold water, whisking until a batter forms.
4. In a separate bowl, whisk together the tempura flour and salt.
5. Heat the oil in a large, deep pot or wok to 375°F.
6. Dip each shrimp and vegetable slice into the batter, then into the tempura flour mixture, ensuring it is well coated.
7. Fry the tempura in the hot oil until golden brown, about 2-3 minutes.
8. Remove with a slotted spoon and drain on paper towels.
9. Place tempura on top of rice in the bento box.
10. Add any desired furikake, pickled vegetables, or seaweed to the side.
11. You can put some fruits and vegetables in the space.

Shogayaki Ginger Pork Bento

Shogayaki ginger pork is a popular dish in Japan that is both delicious and easy to make. Originating from Tokyo, shogayaki means "grilled with ginger," and it's a popular home-cooked meal. The main ingredient in this dish is pork, which is marinated in a simple mixture of soy sauce and other seasonings before being cooked on the stovetop with lots of thinly sliced ginger.

Ingredients:

- 1 pound pork loin, thinly sliced
- 2 tablespoons grated ginger
- 2 cloves garlic, minced
- 1/4 cup soy sauce
- 2 tablespoons brown sugar
- 2 tablespoons mirin
- 1 tablespoon sake
- 2 tablespoons vegetable oil
- 3 cups cooked Japanese-style white rice
- Optional: furikake (rice seasoning), pickled vegetables, and seaweed for packing

Instructions:

1. Mix the ginger, garlic, soy sauce, brown sugar, mirin, and sake in a large bowl.
2. Add the pork slices and marinate for at least 30 minutes or up to 2 hours.
3. In a large pan, heat the vegetable oil over medium-high heat.

4. Drain the pork from the marinade and add to the pan.
5. Cook the pork until browned on both sides and cooked through about 5-7 minutes.
6. Place shogayaki pork on top of the rice in the bento box.
7. Add any desired furikake, pickled vegetables, or seaweed to the side.
8. You can put some fruits and vegetables in the space.

Sesame Ginger Beef Zucchini Noodles

If you're looking for a nutritious, delicious, and easy-to-make meal, look no further than this sesame ginger beef zucchini noodles recipe! With its unique combination of flavors, this dish will surely be a hit with the entire family. It's packed with protein from the beef and nutritious veggie-based noodles that add plenty of fiber and vitamins. Plus, it only takes about 25 minutes to make!

Ingredients:

- 1 pound flank steak, sliced into thin strips
- 2 medium zucchinis, spiralized
- 2 tablespoons canola oil
- 1/4 cup soy sauce
- 1/4 cup brown sugar
- 2 tablespoons rice vinegar
- 2 tablespoons sesame oil
- 2 cloves garlic, minced
- 1 inch ginger, minced
- 2 tablespoons cornstarch
- 2 tablespoons water
- 2 tablespoons toasted sesame seeds
- Optional: sliced green onions and red pepper flakes for packing

Instructions:

1. Whisk together the soy sauce, brown sugar, rice vinegar, sesame oil, garlic, and ginger in a small bowl.

2. Whisk together the cornstarch and water in another small bowl to make a slurry.
3. In a large pan, heat the canola oil over high heat. Add the sliced beef and cook until browned on all sides, about 2-3 minutes.
4. Remove the beef from the pan and set aside.
5. In the same pan, add the zucchini noodles and cook for 2-3 minutes until slightly tender.
6. Add the cooked beef to the pan, the soy sauce mixture, and the cornstarch slurry.
7. Stir until the sauce has thickened and the beef and zucchini noodles are coated about 1-2 minutes.
8. Pack the sesame ginger beef zucchini noodles, garnished with toasted sesame seeds, green onions, and red pepper flakes, into the bento box.
9. Pack additional bento fillers such as salad, vegetables, and fruits.

Sweet & Sour Chicken Bento

Sweet and Sour Chicken is a classic Chinese dish many worldwide enjoy. The combination of sweet and sour flavors makes this dish ideal for those looking for something different from the typical takeout meal. Not only is it delicious, but Sweet and Sour Chicken are also surprisingly easy to make at home. All you need are some simple ingredients, including chicken, bell peppers, vinegar, sugar, and soy sauce, to create a flavorful dish that is sure to please your taste buds.

Ingredients:

- 1 pound boneless, skinless chicken breast cut into bite-sized pieces
- 1 cup flour
- 2 teaspoons baking powder
- 1/2 teaspoon salt
- 1/2 teaspoon black pepper
- 1 egg
- 1/2 cup water
- 3 cups cooked Japanese-style white rice
- 2 tablespoons vegetable oil
- 1 red bell pepper, sliced
- 1 green bell pepper, sliced
- 1 onion, sliced
- 1 cup pineapple chunks
- 1/4 cup apple cider vinegar
- 1/4 cup ketchup
- 3 tablespoons brown sugar

- 2 tablespoons cornstarch
- 2 tablespoons water
- Optional: pickled vegetables and seaweed for packing

Instructions:

1. Whisk together the flour, baking powder, salt, pepper, egg, and water in a large bowl to make a batter.
2. Add the chicken pieces to the batter and sit for 10 minutes.
3. In a large pan, heat the vegetable oil over medium-high heat.
4. Add the chicken pieces to the pan and fry until golden brown, about 5-7 minutes.
5. Remove the chicken from the pan and set aside.
6. Add red and green bell peppers, onion, and pineapple chunks in the same pan.
7. Whisk together the apple cider vinegar, ketchup, brown sugar, cornstarch, and water in a small bowl to make the sweet and sour sauce.
8. Pour the sauce over the vegetables and fruit in the pan.
9. Cook until the sauce has thickened, about 2-3 minutes.
10. Place sweet and sour chicken in the bento box on top of the rice.
11. Add any desired furikake, pickled vegetables, or seaweed to the side.
12. You can put some fruits and vegetables in the space.

Braised Pork Belly Bento

Pork belly is a delicious and versatile cut of meat that can be cooked in many different ways. Braised pork belly is one of the most flavorful and comforting dishes, and it's perfect for a bento box! This article will provide you with an easy-to-follow recipe for braised pork belly bento, as well as a few tips on how to make it even more delicious.

Ingredients:

- 1 pound pork belly, sliced into 1/2-inch pieces
- 1/4 cup soy sauce
- 1/4 cup brown sugar
- 1/4 cup rice vinegar
- 1 tablespoon honey
- 2 cloves garlic, minced
- 1 inch ginger, minced
- 1/2 teaspoon five-spice powder
- 3 cups cooked Japanese-style white rice
- Optional: pickled vegetables and seaweed for packing

Instructions:

1. Whisk together the soy sauce, brown sugar, rice vinegar, honey, garlic, ginger, and five-spice powder in a large pot.
2. Add the sliced pork belly to the pot and bring the mixture to a boil.
3. Reduce heat to low and let the pork belly braise for 45-60 minutes until it is tender and the sauce has thickened.

4. Place braised pork belly on top of rice in the bento box.
5. Add any desired furikake, pickled vegetables, or seaweed to the side.
6. You can put some fruits and vegetables in the space.

BBQ Chicken Sandwiches

BBQ chicken sandwiches are a staple of American cuisine, enjoyed by adults and children. Whether served with potato salad and coleslaw at an outdoor barbecue gathering or as a quick meal on the go, these tasty sandwiches never disappoint. The smoky flavor of the BBQ sauce combined with juicy chicken is a winning combination that can be further enhanced with pickles, onions, and other condiments.

Ingredients:

- 4 boneless, skinless chicken breasts
- 1 cup barbeque sauce
- 4 hamburger buns
- Optional toppings: lettuce, tomato, red onion, cheese, pickles

Instructions:

1. Preheat your grill or grill pan to medium-high heat.
2. Season the chicken breasts with salt and pepper.
3. Place the chicken on the grill or pan and cook for 5-6 minutes on each side until the internal temperature reaches 165°F.
4. During the last few minutes of cooking, brush the chicken breasts with the barbeque sauce.
5. Toast the hamburger buns on the grill or in a toaster.
6. Assemble the sandwiches by placing the cooked chicken breast on the bottom bun and adding your desired toppings, such as lettuce, tomato, red onion, cheese, and pickles.

7. Spread more barbeque sauce on the top bun and place it on the sandwich.
8. Pack the sandwich in a bento box and put some fruits and vegetables in the space.

Spinach Feta Grilled Cheese Sandwiches

Grilled cheese sandwiches are a classic comfort food that everyone loves. Perfect for lunch or dinner, these sandwiches can be made in various ways. The spinach feta grilled cheese sandwich is a delicious take on this staple dish. This tasty sandwich is easy to make and packed with flavor. Feta cheese and baby spinach add a creamy texture and nutty flavor, making it a fantastic way to upgrade your grilled cheese sandwich game.

Ingredients:

- 4 slices of whole-grain bread
- 4 oz of crumbled feta cheese
- 2 cups of fresh spinach leaves
- 4 tablespoons of butter, softened
- Optional: additional seasonings such as garlic powder or red pepper flakes

Instructions:

1. Preheat a large skillet or griddle over medium heat.
2. Spread 1 tablespoon of butter on one side of each slice of bread.
3. Place the bread, butter-side down, in the skillet or griddle.
4. On two slices of bread, sprinkle a handful of crumbled feta cheese.
5. On top of the cheese, place a handful of fresh spinach leaves.

6. Optional: sprinkle with seasonings such as garlic powder or red pepper flakes.
7. Top the spinach with the remaining slices of bread, with the butter side facing up.
8. Cook the sandwiches until the bread is golden brown, approximately 3-4 minutes on each side.
9. Once the sandwiches are done, remove them from the heat and let them cool for a few minutes before slicing them in half and packing them.
10. Pack the sandwich in a bento box and put some fruits and vegetables in the space.

Printed in Great Britain
by Amazon

24927578R00040